54

MISSOURI
Faces and Places

MISSOURI
Faces and Places

Wes Lyle

Photographer

John Hall

Writer

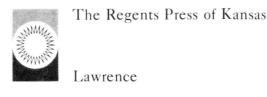

The Regents Press of Kansas

Lawrence

Standard Book Number 0-7006-0165-1

Library of Congress Catalog Card Number 77-081508

Printed in the United States of America

Designed by Kathryn Hanson Lyle

For Kay Lyle

For Larry and Winifred Hall

Preface

This photographic odyssey began several years ago. It required thousands of miles of travel, which gave me the chance to explore many facets of a state diverse in its beauty and people.

Some of the persons pictured are friends of mine. Most are total strangers. All have a certain pride and dignity as they go about their daily lives.

Here, then, are my impressions of Missouri. It is by nature a very personal look at the state. Some are fleeting impressions, others lasting, but all are very real. I hope you will find something you have not seen before.

Wes Lyle

Introduction

Missouri is an ancient place. Like the confluence of its two great rivers, Missouri has been a mixing place since the first winds began to blow and time began. Reading the story written on the land by the wind and the rivers, we know a place washed by seas and glaciers; a land whose first creatures left themselves as limestone in the evolutionary melt of time. Missouri was land for the first time as the seas receded and the Ozark hills emerged about 500,000,000 years ago.

At one time, the seas over Missouri were filled with sharks. Today the sea flowers can be found as fossils in the rock along the creeks of many hill farms. Surely it must add to the thrill of this place called Missouri to know that the Gulf of Mexico reached into the lowland counties of the Bootheel a mere 140,000,000 years ago; to know that dinosaurs trudged through those Bootheel swamps.

When the last glaciers had pushed their boulders down from the north as far as the Missouri River, when the seas had gone for the last time, the land we call Missouri was ready for man. The time between then and now has been a time of evolutionary adventure.

The Ozarks were already there, among the oldest hills on the North American continent. In fact, the Appalachian, Mexican, and Ozark plateaus are the only areas on the North American continental mainland that have not been flooded or glaciated for 500,000,000 years. Parts of Missouri have been around for a long time. In the valleys of those Ozark hills you can follow the story of evolution in the flora and fauna from then until now.

Missouri is a land where the glacial region north of the Missouri River reaches down to meet the southwest prairie, the eastern edge of a vast and sloping plain that extends from the Rocky Mountains. The ancient, and sometimes mysterious, Ozark region extends from the prairie to the southeast Missouri lowlands, the northern reach of a broad alluvial plain that runs to the Gulf of Mexico.

Missouri is a place of biological edges, a place of incredible diversity. That diversity ranges in wildlife from the blind cavefish to the black bear still foraging in the heavy forests; from the prehistoric-looking pileated woodpecker to the great bald eagle. Wildflowers, grasses, trees, animals, and man depend on this diversity for survival. Each species seeks some edge or niche and, finding its own unique food and shelter, is able to survive.

Think of Missouri, for a moment, as a nation of grasses. Twelve of the fourteen tribes of the grass family found in the United States can be found as native Missouri species. Their names read like a poem:

Brome, fescue, milo, manna grass.
Bluegrass, lovegrass, fowl meadow-grass.
Bluestem, purpletop, wild oats, and rye.
Silverbeard, bluejoint, and nodding foxtail.

In among the grasses blooms a paradise of wildflowers—as many wildflowers as there are faces in the crowds of Missouri's diversity of people.

Missouri was the meeting place of the two greatest families of Indian tribes in all North America, the Algonquin and the Sioux. To the Sioux belong the closely related Osage, Missouri, Kansas, Iowa, and Arkansas tribes. To the Algonquin belong the Fox Indians, among many others. When the warriors of the Fox encountered the warriors of the Missouri tribe, the state was named. The Fox came back to their fires talking of the "mesisi-piya" (Mississippi), which, in Fox language, meant "Big River." They spoke also of the "Big-Canoe People" who dwelt at the confluence of the two great rivers. The Fox word for "Big-Canoe People" was "Missouri." The fleeing Missouri Indians escaped annihilation at the hands of Fox warriors by paddling up the river in big canoes. They called themselves "Niutachi," or "People Who Dwell at the Mouth of the River." Their Sioux word for that river was "Nishodse," which means "muddy water."

The Big-Canoe People moved up the river just as others moved west.
It is not difficult to imagine a migration of canoes pushing up the Osage
and the Des Moines and the Arkansas rivers. They moved slowly, no doubt,
as you and I would move today if we were paddling up streams from place
to place needing only food and firewood. When the white man came,
those same rivers and streams were trade routes and then arteries of the
new migration.

Wes Lyle begins his book of photographs in St. Louis, where the
settlement of Missouri by white men began. St. Louis, St. Charles, and
Ste. Genevieve, perhaps the oldest, were names given the first towns by
their French settlers.

Before 1800, Missouri's white population clustered in small settlements
along the Mississippi River. With the Louisiana Purchase in 1804,
extensive migration and settlement of the state began westward along
the Missouri River.

The first Missourians are said to have come from Virginia, North Carolina,
Kentucky, and Tennessee. They left the rugged terrain of their
Appalachian Mountains and traveled across half the nation to the Missouri
hill country. There is some historic suggestion that those among them
known as the Scotch-Irish settled in the rugged Appalachians in the first
place because the land reminded them of the place they left for America.
They were a hardy bunch, wherever they came from.

One student of the English language suggests that a "good ole Missouri
hill twang" accent may be the closest anyone today can come to hearing
the language of England as Shakespeare heard it when he wrote.
That is speculation that might not sit well with Shakespearean scholars
or Missouri hill folk, but the language and music have interesting
similarities.

North of the Missouri River, for the most part, the people came
to Missouri from New England, New York, Pennsylvania, and Ohio.
They were a people from different terrain, with a different temperament.
More than a few Missourians can trace their lineage back to a mix of
Pennsylvania Dutch on one side and Scotch-Irish on the other.

The migration, like the crisscrossing paths of the animal herds, was both movement and mixture. The signs of that migration can be seen everywhere: in places like Weston in northwestern Missouri where some of the finest tobacco in the world is grown; in towns along the Missouri River east of Jefferson City built on terrain similar to the river valleys of Germany.

Missouri is a place of wildflowers and mysterious caves carved out of ancient rock by underground rivers. Missouri is a place where a nation of grasses gathers in tribes; where tribes of Indians met; where glaciated land meets prairie; where prairie meets Ozark highlands; where rugged hills meet the Mississippi embayment, not long ago a cypress swamp. Missouri is a place where sea flowers have yielded to wildflowers whose beauty and diversity are a fitting song to the beauty and diversity of Missouri's people.

Missouri can be seen best, perhaps, in the faces of its people: faces that show all man knows; faces that show, like Missouri bluffs, the carving of the winds and the journey of the rivers; faces that read like time and place. The beauty of it all is open for everyone to see. Nothing here is beyond our vision. Nothing in the universe is beyond that vision.

The far fields of wildflowers, like the faces, reach back to a time before there were places, back to when Missouri began, and forward beyond the parade of man through Missouri's fields and forests to a time when only the wind will remember.

John M. Hall

Thank You

. . . to my father, H. V. Lyle

. . . Johnny Blevans

. . . Bill Baker, President, *The Kansas City Star;*
Bob Pearman, Managing Editor, *The Kansas City Times;*
Casey Jones, Assistant Managing Editor, *The Kansas City Times;*
Paul Haskins, City Editor, *The Kansas City Times;*
Ken Paik, Photo Editor, *The Kansas City Times*

. . . to my fellow staff members on *The Kansas City Times:*
Peter Allen, Bill Batson, Joe Coleman, George Olson,
Bill Sims, and David Winger

. . . Jim Weishar

. . . to Mary Ann and Sean Hall

. . . to all who believe

. . . to the people of Missouri.

MISSOURI
Faces and Places

"In the province of the mind, what one
believes to be true is true or becomes true.
In the province of the mind there are no limits."

John Lilly
Center of the Cyclone

St. Louis on the west bank of the Mississippi River

Man is capable of a limitless vision. The ability of our minds to imagine, together with the ability of our hands to build, allows man to dream his future and build that future according to his imaginings.

A city like St. Louis can be thought of as a kind of culmination of the visions and dreams of many men. A city grows, as St. Louis did, from such meager dreams as the building of a log cabin on the west banks of the Mississippi River in 1764, where Pierre Laclede and Auguste Chouteau opened their fur-trading post.

On the banks of the Mississippi River at St. Louis, surrounded by a twentieth-century metropolis, we can look back at what came before us down the long river of geologic time, and we can look off toward the future and wonder which of man's imaginings will become reality in the year 2000 and beyond.

If future man comes upon this stainless-steel arch, the result of one man's imaginings, he will have some notion of our dreams for the future. Stand under the Gateway Arch some full-moon night and listen as it reaches toward the stars and returns with their light. The arch is also a tribute to the dreams of our past: to the dreams of men like Thomas Jefferson, who negotiated the purchase of the Louisiana Territory; to the dreams of the explorers with Lewis and Clark, who headed west up the Missouri River in May 1804. After more than two years and 7,000 miles, they brought back word of the Pacific Ocean.

Measure the speed of jets across America today against the years since 1804. Man's imagination propels him quickly into the future.

Man has always been an explorer adventuring out beyond the circle of fire, out beyond the flat maps of ancient cartographers marked with warnings that read "Here Be Monsters," out beyond the pull of earth's gravity. Man's future has first been man's dream of that future.

The Gateway Arch framing the Old Courthouse at St. Louis

The Old Courthouse seen in reflection

The dream of Dred Scott who sought his freedom in the Old Courthouse at St. Louis in 1847 could well have been a dream of freedom for all black men.

Downtown St. Louis

Not all man's dreams bring him to a new world. The dreams of youth
often become the rememberings of old men.

Flower vendor

Between dream and memory, we find the beauty of simple things:
Red carnations, fresh-cut asparagus.

Soulard Market

Most of our dreams play out in day-to-day places like the Soulard Market, where Ulysses S. Grant once sold cordwood as a young farmer, or in the row houses of the Soulard District near the Church of Saints Peter and Paul of the Holy Apostle.

The Soulard District

Although most dreams are tied to everyday lives, we all feel the pull
of something more. For some it is bright lights and big city. For some,
a freight train whistle going down the night. For almost every man,
there is the pull of the river to the sea.

River boats fill the dreams of our wandering as they filled the dreams of
the boy from Hannibal who became Mark Twain. Today men pursue the
same romance of the river from the wheelhouses of diesel-powered
towboats that push strings of barges as long as a quarter of a mile up and
down the rivers of the world. Same river, same dream, different machines.

The mooring rings will outlast man, and the granite blocks of the levee
will outlast the rings, but not the river.

Levee at St. Louis

Towboat tied off
at St. Louis

Towboat crew at Jefferson City

River men say they like the pay and the food, and even the work.
But it's the lure of the river that brings them back when they've worked
their thirty days on and taken their thirty days off.

Somewhere in every river man's mind there must be a picture of fog
lifting and the feel of diesel engines as the boat heads down river into
the morning sun.

Missouri River below Kansas City

Deck hand

On the river, like everywhere else, there is the day-to-day business of
deck hands using cheater bars on ratchet handles tightening down steel
cables, called wires, that tie a string of barges together to make a tow.

Some men do their dreaming on smaller rivers. Thoreau said: "Some men fish all their lives without knowing it is not really the fish they are after."

Bank fisherman, Little Platte River

The river is the source of life and the source of the mystery of our
beginnings. As water, the river gives food and drink. As a place of mystery,
the water holds answers that link us to our past in creatures like
the gar, the paddlefish, and the sturgeon. Just as surely as water is a place
of beginnings, the river holds secrets that anticipate our future.

Missouri River at Lexington

Man has cast his nets and lines into rivers as long as there has been man, and rivers before him. When man is gone, the rains will come and carry his dust to the rivers, and the rivers will flow with the memory of his passing.

River's harvest

Tom Bogdon and longnose gar

The flow of rains and underground rivers eventually hollows out those caverns in the earth called caves. Ask those who go exploring there what it is they go searching for. Those who explore Missouri's many caves bring out descriptions of strange creatures like the blind white cavefish that locate food and enemies using a highly developed sensitivity to movements in the water. Others come out of caves lacking words to describe the absolute darkness, the complete absence of light.

As in all explorations into the unfamiliar, caves can be the place where one encounters cavefish, or new dimensions of the self.

Caves are places where time is measured in thousands of years as the slow flow of a natural solution of carbonic acid seeps into cracks and eats away the rock, leaving a sediment finally carried away by underground streams. Not all of time moves at the same speed.

Onondaga Cave, Crawford County

Ice stalagmites

Sheep Cave in the Meramec River valley

Green's Cave,
Crawford County

Bonnot's Mill

Small towns open like flowers, unfolding from out-of-the-way places to reveal a kind of beauty and harmony not found anywhere else. Here one can see the values of human existence, can sense the intricate cooperation and communication among creatures inching their way along the path of civilizations.

The day begins with clean light, with the sound of birds not lost in the noise of larger places. The first footsteps are those of a boy and his dog delivering the morning newspaper. The sounds of good morning.

In small towns you can still hear the sound of a screen door opening, the sound of a broom sweeping the sidewalk, the sound of porch swings in the evening.

The sights and sounds blend into something that is more than things seen or heard, something you can walk into and know. Small towns hold a quiet joy.

Sunday morning, Weston

Poplar Bluff Fire Department

Street dance near the
Pony Express Stables,
St. Joseph

Bicentennial
wagon train

Fourth of July, 1976

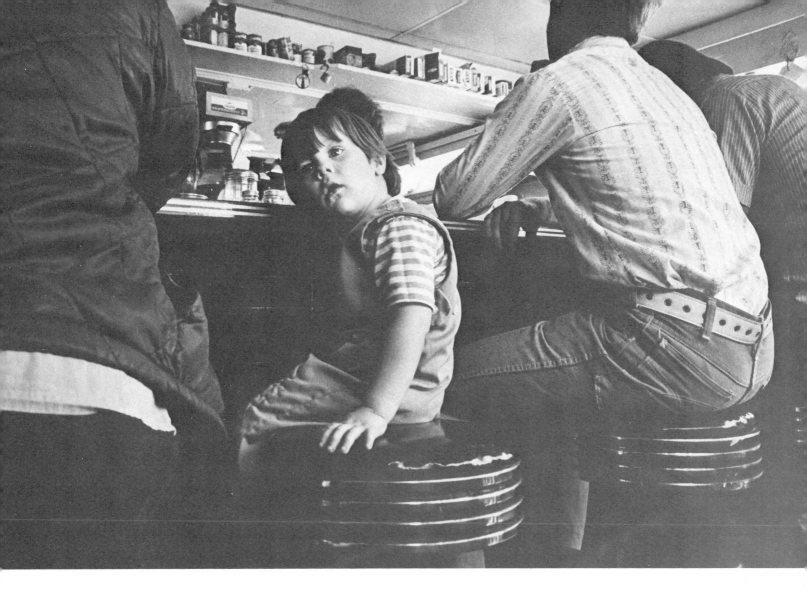

Lunchtime, Lexington

The beauty of a place, or a way of life, can best be seen in the faces of the people. If you forget the wonder of it all, look in the faces of the children.

After school

The ritual of daily lives that pass through places like small-town grocery stores is a kind of prayer: the quiet joy of children buying a piece of candy after school; the smell of fresh onions; the memories of old women who have put a thousand thoughts on their shelves, and then given those thoughts away.

Stephens Grocery, Rushville

The Mark Twain Museum and home seen from
Becky Thatcher's bedroom window, Hannibal

Did you ever watch the walk of a young boy? His walk displays the
sense of importance he feels in his early years. The dreams of small boys
often grow with them to become a sense of importance in a larger world.
It depends on the dream.

Such were the dreams of Mark Twain as young Sam Clemens in
Hannibal. Such were the dreams of the young Truman, who never lost
that sense of himself. Both men came from small towns where, perhaps,
young boys have a better chance to build dreams they can hold on to.

The home of Harry and Bess Truman, Independence

Ravenswood, Cooper County

Sometimes the dreams of greatness and importance get passed down generations of children until one day there is a great mansion filled with the portraits and legends of those who pursued those dreams. Ravenswood mansion south of Boonville is such a place. In 1839, Nathaniel Leonard, founder of Ravenswood, established what was to become an internationally famous herd of Shorthorn cattle.
The Leonard ancestors reach back through a Missouri Supreme Court justice, a commander of Fort Niagara during the War of 1812, a chaplain in George Washington's army, a minister at Plymouth, Massachusetts.

Front porch, Lexington

Lafayette County judges: Harvey Day, C. L. Summers, and August Rasa

Pony Express Memorial, St. Joseph

The legacy of Missouri in the short history of America is richer than many
know. Missouri's sons include men who have led the nation, the army,
international corporations. The list is long and filled with famous men, some
famous outlaws. The exploration of much of what has become America
began in Missouri with expeditions like the one led by Lewis and Clark,
or with brief episodes of adventure like the Pony Express. On April 3, 1860,
a Pony Express rider left St. Joseph on the first leg of the 2,000- mile route
to Sacramento, California. The distance could be covered in eight days
of hard riding with riders changing horses every ten to fifteen miles.

World War I Memorial, Polk County Courthouse, Bolivar

Wentworth Military Academy, Lexington

In many towns, Missouri's heritage is preserved in one way or another. A cannon ball lodged in the northeast column of the Lafayette County Courthouse at Lexington was fired during the Civil War Battle of Lexington in September 1861. After fifty-two hours of fighting, the Union troops surrendered to the Confederate invaders under General Sterling Price who took 3,000 prisoners and broke the chain of Union-held posts along the Missouri River.

Jasper County Courthouse, Carthage

It was no accident that George Caleb Bingham chose Arrow Rock as
the place where he would live and paint the Missouri he knew. Or that
Thomas Hart Benton would come home to Missouri to find the subjects
of his life-long work as a painter in the rich legacy of his own people.
Benton died in his studio the night he completed a mural called *Country
Music*. It was Benton who said: "The only way an artist can personally
fail is to quit." Such is the legacy of every man, artist or laborer.

Man's time on earth is a brief interlude in the turning of the universe.
If we measure time in man years, life is short. If we measure time
on a calendar of granite engraved by the wind and the river, man's life
becomes a time of precious hours like the lives of butterflies and moths.

The granite that forms the Johnson Shut-Ins southwest of Ironton in
Reynolds County is Pre-Cambrian rhyolite cooled from lava 1.5 billion
years ago.

Johnson Shut-Ins

Farm pond swimming hole, Jackson County

Meramec River

Beaver Creek, Taney County

Edwards Mill, School of the Ozarks, Point Lookout

Millstone center

Hodgson Mill,
Ozark County

For the young, the hours pass like days. For the not so young, the minutes seem to increase with a velocity approaching the speed of light. And yet, wise men say, man can live a lifetime in an hour, can see the universe in a grain of sand.

Up and down the long rows of cotton that reach from the Missouri Bootheel into the Deep South, time is the creeping shadow of the sun.

Picking cotton near Cooter in Pemiscot County

Weighing cotton

Field workers near Kennett, going home

Hanging clothes

"Peace like a river so gently is flowing, how sweet to my soul is this marvelous peace." The words to the chorus of this hymn sung over and over might well have come to its first singer at the end of a long day with humility of hard work felt in his bones, his tired feet in the river.

Cooling off in a Bootheel canal

The beauty of wildflowers and butterflies is an expression of their incredible diversity. Their beauty is a result of their freedom to grow as an expression of their individuality. If each man grew in such freedom, would man's diversity become as beautiful as the wildflowers and the butterflies?

Communal living at East Wind, Tecumseh

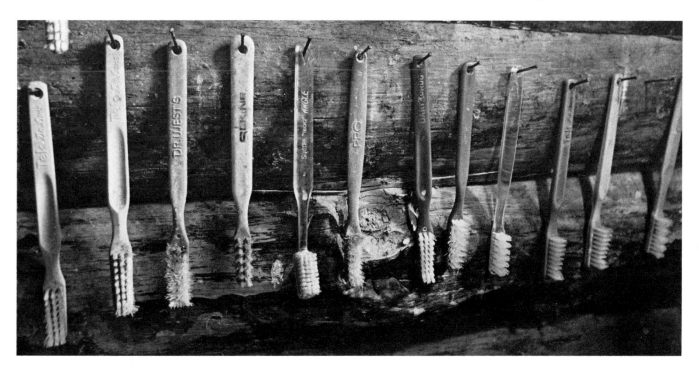

A new building
at East Wind

Wildflowers grow with wildflowers. Butterflies fly with butterflies among
the wildflowers. Similarities of mind and need hold them together in
smaller worlds within worlds. Within any circle there is room for a smaller
circle.

Man gathers together in the same sort of way. Neanderthal man gathered
around a fire. Twentieth-century man often gathers around an idea.
It is the same sort of gathering. Smaller circles within the larger circles
of society allow men to live in different ways, to express different lives
that can be as diverse and beautiful as the wildflowers and the butterflies.

Who can say which differences among the lives of men will eventually
become the difference that allows man to survive?

And so we go down the paths of diversity driven by individual minds
and individual needs toward who knows what, or where, or why.

Sister Mary Claudia, rural nurse, visits Paul Witt near Willow Springs

The United Church of Christ, Wellington

Some men live in groups. Some men live alone. Some men find
most of their answers within themselves. Some rely on sources outside
themselves. In every man's life there is a time when he asks the question
"Why?" and hears no answer, asks again and hears only a stillness in
the sky. Maybe he kneels down in the woods, or in a church. Maybe
his kneeling is a simple act to get closer to the earth, or an act in unison
with others trying to lift their minds to a god for some answer beyond
themselves. The ritual is the same: a reckoning with the unknown. The
manifestations of that ritual differ in degree depending on man's need to
pray alone in the woods, or with others in cathedrals.

The source of the answer makes no difference. Each man hears whatever
he hears within himself and must get up and go on, or lie down and die.

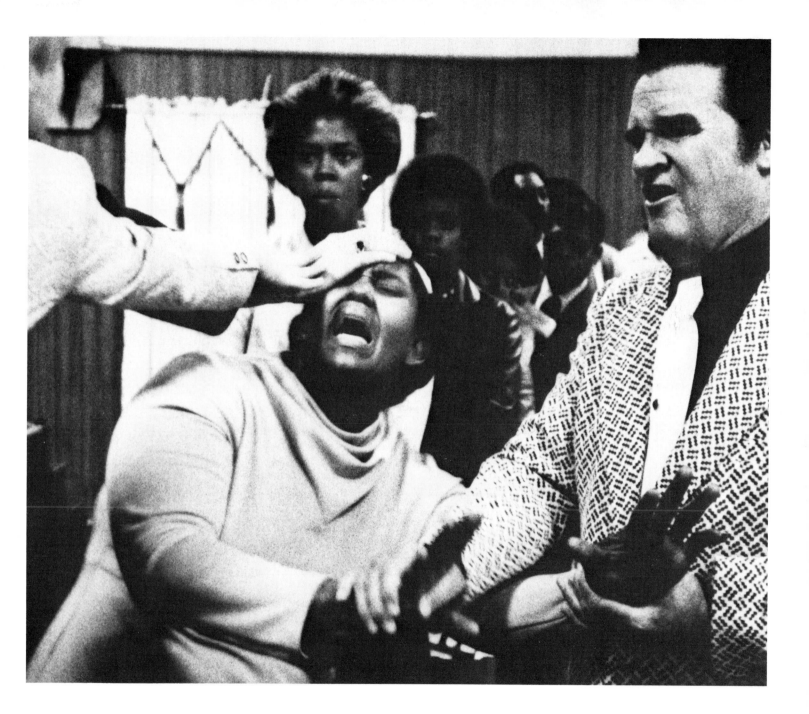

Faith healer

Brush arbor revival, Sparta

Calling on the Lord

The land is a dance to the sounds of a universe that is the source of all our joy. Man is so closely tied to the land, such a part of it, that he lives in unison with its natural rhythms whether he dances with the turning of the earth, or turns the other way. It is still the dance of the earth that man follows.

Man's rhythms are the pulsations of living matter. Man's life moves in cycles like the turning of the earth through the seasons. The major movements in man's life repeat larger movements.

In winter when the land is quiet, man is quiet. In spring when the land is bursting, man is bursting with new joy. It is a time of new beginnings, a time of plantings. The wave of nostalgia that fills man in the final light of autumn, the pull toward home he feels with the falling leaves, is the call of the land heard by every living thing.

Within those seasons there are smaller cycles. Every month the tides run full in the pull of the moon. The mammoth seas respond just as the blood in the capillaries of the human body responds when the moon is full.

Science has just begun to chart the basic forces that influence man's metabolism and his behavior. But any man whose body and mind are tuned to the universe knows he repeats the rhythms of his earth, knows that he is just as much liquid as the universe is sea, that he is just as much body as the universe is land. Some things man knows without being told. How does the fisherman know when a sea storm is coming? Old timers literally "have a feeling" in their bones as their bodies respond to changes in barometric pressure. The human organism can be just as sensitive as the plant that turns toward the light of the sun and closes in upon itself in sleep with the coming of darkness.

Man moves from the still point of conception to the still point of death in a dance of circles with the turning of the universe.

Howell County

Preparing river bottom land, Orchard Farm, St. Charles County

Fall, Meramec River valley

This is the time
when robins disappear.
Haze fills the valleys.
Afternoon light is different.
I discover past lives,
scarlet berries on the dogwood,
persimmons not quite ripe.

One night the wind changes.
The voice of an owl
gives way to a sound
coming down the night
a fast freight.

The morning is grey; breeze steady
north northeast. The robin is gone.

Lunar halo

Table Rock Reservoir

Looking south off Taum Sauk Mountain

The Coming of Winter

Winds tell the sparrows
to flee.
Crows fly lower.

An old man knows,
hands at his throat
to hold the collar closed.

Quail gather
in a circle,
tails together:

One mind
listening
for the hunter.

Platte County farm

Slight Changes in the Song

The old man is gone:
from the wooden gates
he swung open
every morning of the year;
from his sound
that brought the mares
to the barn
to nose clean the oats
in the feed boxes
while he stood in out of the wind.

And now the ritual wind returns
moving up the creek bed through the valleys
and on up through this farm
until it rounds his barn
and rattles the weathered wooden gates
and turns the mares, nose into the wind.

Storm

The changing sound
moves the grain,
a wind of whispers
precise with the fear
of butterflies.

The white barn
rides the ridge.
Its lightning rods
are prairie women
waiting naked for the rains.

Tobacco barn near Weston

Joy of Flowers Opening

Your eyes, a deep and calling blue.
The calm, a soft touch
that soothes the soul.
The quiet clean with the breeze
of your voice and my listening.

I practice the ritual
by holding a stone
from the spring-fed stream.
I am learning the stone's calm
moving inside its quiet
toward the flight of the universe.

Queen Anne's lace

Shooting star, Taney County

Dogwood, Ozark County stream

American woodcock

Snow geese, Squaw Creek National Wildlife Refuge

There are many paths—
as many as there are
bird tracks in the snow.
If you wish to arrive,
choose only those
that come back to yourself.

Young great horned owl

Immature bald eagle,
great horned owl,
red-tailed hawk

White-tailed doe

Green-winged teal

Morning Watch

In the quiet hour
when the sounds of night listen
for the sounds of day,
fog rises unseen in the valleys.

A barn owl in cedar moves the damp air
with its round and centering voice.
The owl stops.
It feels the watching.

A slight change,
the sigh of cedar limb,
the owl outdistances the darkness.

A tight wire fence of silence
holds the air in refrain.

The nighthawk makes one last foray
down the edge of light,
then goes for a dark hole in the forest.
The bird plummets in
releasing the voice of a crow.

It is the blue heron who answers,
his color returning.

Great blue heron

A Poem in the Night for Mary Ann with Child

My woman wonders,
with the dew,
if the beauty within her
will be as full
as the open rose
while first light soothes the sky,
still fraught with night,
like a willow breeze;
and the rose unfolds.

The song of life that is man among all living things began like the unfolding of a rose in the breeze of first light. Imagine standing on a hill overlooking the cradle of civilization, a rich valley from which man would come. Imagine hearing the song of the first creature. And then the chorus of another species, and another. Imagine hearing the song grow like the legion of voices that begins with the voice of one cicada on an August evening and becomes a symphony of summer sounds greater than the darkness.

If you could foreshorten the slowly developing song of evolution into one summer evening, and if you were standing on a hill where the air was so pure you could hear everything for hundreds of miles, when it came time in that evening for the song of man to join the chorus of all living things for the first time, you would remember.

We all remember that first sound of man among other creatures in the valley of living things. We know this, and all things that have come before us, in a way not much different from the handing down of stories from one generation to another. In the story of our beginnings, and in the adventures of evolution, we know the things we know in a way we can never forget.

When we die, our minds become diffused in the flow of earth and underground rivers. Everything we know becomes part of the universe. And everything that grows from that universe after us knows what we know.

It is as simple as the flow from a spring to the creek to the stream to the river to the ocean, where the sun draws up the water and the wind carries it back over the land to fall and become a spring again. The river knows what each rivulet that has become the river knows.

It is in this way, or a way very much like this, that man knows all that man has ever known. In the valley of our beginnings, where the air is pure and dry, where sound travels like light into forever, the song of man continues.

We must look closely into the eyes of those around us to know the beauty of their lives.

Amish children

Heading home

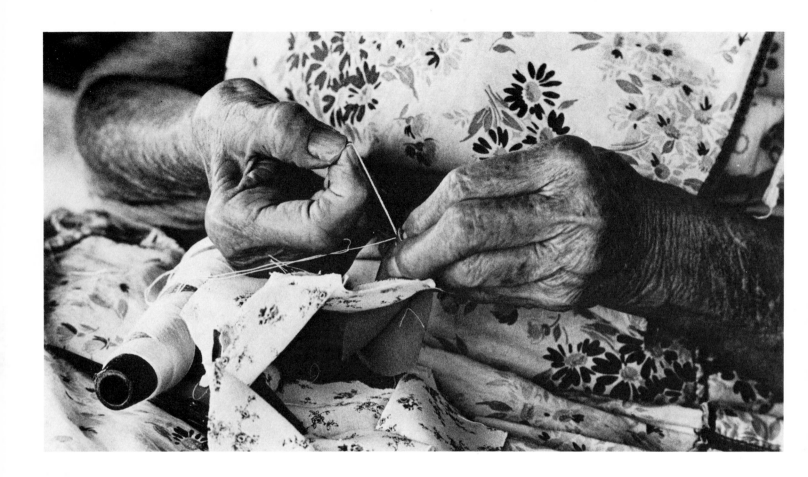

Quilting

Lane's General Store

Lester Anderson, Weston

Harold and Rosella Boss, Chamois

Mr. and Mrs. Alfred Swaringam and grandchild, Arcadia

Proud and simple living in the Ozark hills

Herman Liepard, Platte City

James Icenhower, Cedar County

Kerrie Ann Grimm, Chamois

We see more, somehow, in the eyes of children and in the eyes of those who have walked the circle of their lives and come back to that place of beginnings where we allow ourselves the simple joy of being.   It is in these eyes that look without judging and see without preconception that we find the purest expression of the joy called living.

Marriah Wall, Liberty

New puppy

The Wee Bunny Ranch, Texas County

John Hall, Cole County

Plowing near
Higginsville

The light of each man's vision comes from his eyes, spreads out from his face: to his hands that take up the work of his dream; to his feet that carry him through the dance of his imaginings.

Each man must dance to the music of his own song.

Edgar Williams, Higginsville

You're lookin' at the oldest horse trainer in these hills. Frank Hodges, 91, Ocie

Tobacco warehouse, Weston

The Cooper County Anti-Theft Association

Catfish and Irene at the High Chaparral Tavern

George Osborn, Osborn's Saloon, Weston

Country music

Roundhouse stoker

Gandy dancer

Beans

Day's end

I don't get along with people. I don't like their ways.
I just grow a garden and stay in these hills. Ozark hermit

Banjo music

Bettye Miller and Milt Abel

Where the rivers, and the faces, and the streets, and the straight lines of
steel come together, there is another city rising up from man's imaginings.
The essence of this place is a mingling of its fountains and its jazz.
Kansas City, on the edge of the prairie, looks off into the future from
different beginnings. It has its own particular sound and light.

Mutual Musicians Foundation Hall,
Kansas City

Muse of the Missouri, Ninth and Main

The song of Kansas City begins along the banks of the Missouri and the Kaw. It lingers in the railroad yards where hoboes pause in journeys that go off in all directions. It flows in a stream of light that began with the first expeditions, and moves today with the speed of freeways.

Construction

The song of Kansas City echoes like the blues among the cool shadows of its buildings. It rises, like the cry of the newspaper vendor in the concrete canyons of Tenth and Main, to the towers of imagination that command a better view of a sky meant for dreaming; a sky where man flies just ahead of vapor trails in machines that catch the last glint of light from a sun already shining on the back side of another world.

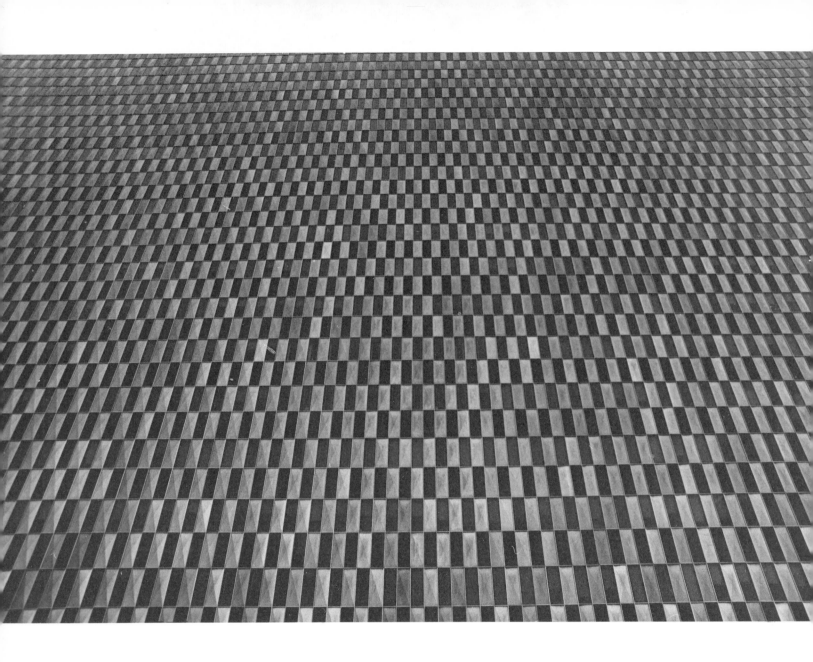

Federal Office Building, Kansas City

New York Life Building

Petticoat Lane

Twelfth Street

Auctioneer's school

American Royal Grand Champion

Show horses

A winner at the American Royal

Flag Day

Black Muslim children

Loose Park

Christmas at Crown Center

Christmas lights, Country Club Plaza

Fountain, Alameda Plaza Hotel

Kansas City